Copyright © 2024

Illustrator - Creative Designer: Valentina VAROL

No part of this publication may be reproduced, stored in a retrieval system, or transmitted in any from or by any means, electronic, mechanical, photocopying, recording, or otherwise, without written permission of the publisher.